Spurgeon on Baptism
Three Essential Sermons

Charles H. Spurgeon

Bibliographical Information

This volume is a collection of sermons delivered by Charles Spurgeon (1834–1892) between 1864 and 1889. His writings were originally published in book form by Passmore & Alabaster in London, England in the late nineteenth century.

an Ichthus Publications edition

ISBN 10: 1500851744
ISBN 13: 978-1500851743

www.ichthuspublications.com

Contents

1

Baptism—A Burial

October 30, 1881
Metropolitan Tabernacle, Newington

"Know ye not, that so many of us as were baptized into Jesus Christ were baptized into his death? Therefore we are buried with him by baptism into death: that like as Christ was raised up from the dead by the glory of the Father, even so we also should walk in newness of life."

—Romans 6:3-4

I SHALL NOT ENTER INTO controversy over this text, although over it some have raised the question of infant baptism or believers' baptism, immersion or sprinkling. If any person can give a consistent and instructive interpretation of the text, otherwise than by assuming believers' immersion to be Christian baptism, I should like to see them do it. I myself am quite incapable of performing such a feat, or even of imagining how it can be done. I am content to take the view that baptism signifies the burial of believers in water in the name of the Lord, and I shall so interpret the text. If any think not so, it may at least interest them to know what we understand to be the meaning of the baptismal rite, and I trust that they may think none the less of the spiritual sense because they differ as to the external sign. After all, the visible emblem is not the most prominent matter in the text. May God the Holy Spirit help us to reach its inner teaching.

I do not understand Paul to say that if improper persons, such as unbelievers, and hypocrites, and deceivers, are baptized they are baptized into our Lord's death. He says "so many of us," putting himself with the rest of the children of God. He intends such as are entitled to baptism, and come to it with their hearts in a right state. Of them he says, "Know ye not, that so many of us as were baptized into Jesus Christ were baptized into his death?" He does not even intend to say that those who were rightly baptized have all of them entered into the fullness of its spiritual meaning; for if they had, there would have been no need of the question, "Know ye not?" It would seem that some had been baptized who did not clearly know the meaning of their own baptism. They had faith, and a glimmer of knowledge sufficient to make them right recipients of baptism, but they

5

were not well instructed in the teaching of baptism; perhaps they saw in it only a washing, but had never discerned the burial. I will go further, and say that I question if any of us yet know the fullness of the meaning of either of the ordinances which Christ has instituted. As yet we are, with regard to spiritual things, like children playing on the beach while the ocean rolls before us. At best we wade up to our ankles like our little ones on the sea shore. A few among us are learning to swim; but then we only swim where the bottom is almost within reach. Who among us has yet come to lose sight of shore and to swim in the Atlantic of divine love, where fathomless truth rolls underneath, and the infinite is all around? Oh, may God daily teach us more and more of what we already know in part, and may the truth which we have as yet but dimly perceived come to us in a brighter and clearer manner, till we see all things in clear sunlight. This can only be as our own character becomes more clear and pure; for we see according to what we are; and as is the eye such is that which it sees. The pure in heart alone can see a pure and holy God. We shall be like Jesus when we shall see him as he is, and certainly we shall never see him as he is till we are like him. In heavenly things we see as much as we have within ourselves. He who has eaten Christ's flesh and blood spiritually is the man who can see this in the sacred Supper, and he who has been baptized into Christ sees Christ in baptism. To him that hath shall be given, and he shall have abundantly.

Baptism sets forth the death, burial, and resurrection of Christ, and our participation therein. Its teaching is twofold. First, think of *our representative union with Christ*, so that when he died and was buried it was on our behalf, and we were thus buried with him. This will give you the teaching of baptism so far as it sets forth a creed. We declare in baptism that we believe in the death of Jesus, and desire to partake in all the merit of it. But there is a second equally important matter and that is *our realized union with Christ* which is set forth in baptism, not so much as a doctrine of our creed as a matter of our experience. There is a manner of dying, of being buried, of rising, and of living in Christ which must be displayed in each one of us if we are indeed members of the body of Christ.

I. First, then, I want you to think of OUR REPRESENTATIVE UNION WITH CHRIST as it is set forth in baptism as a truth to be believed. Our Lord Jesus is the substitute for his people, and when he died it was on their behalf and in their stead. The great doctrine of our justification lies in this, that Christ took our sins, stood in our place, and as our surety suffered, and bled, and died, thus presenting on our behalf a sacrifice for sin. We are to regard him, not as a private person, but as our representative. We are buried with him in baptism unto death to show that we accept him as being for us dead and buried.

Baptism as a burial with Christ signifies, first, *acceptance of the death and burial of Christ as being for us*. Let us do that at this very moment with all our hearts. What other hope have we? When our divine Lord came down from the heights of glory and took upon himself our manhood, he became one with you and with me; and being found in fashion as a man, it pleased the Father to lay sin upon him, even your sins and mine. Do you not accept that truth, and agree that the Lord Jesus should be the bearer of your guilt, and stand for you in the sight of God? "Amen! Amen!" say all of you. He went up to the tree loaded with all this guilt, and there he suffered in our room and stead as we ought to have suffered. It pleased the Father, instead of bruising us, to bruise him. He put him to grief, making his soul an offering for sin. Do we not gladly accept Jesus as our substitute? O beloved, whether you have been baptized in water or not, I put this question to you, "Do you accept the Lord Jesus as your surety and substitute?" For if you do not, you shall bear your own guilt and carry your own sorrow, and stand in your own place beneath the glance of the angry justice of God. Many of us at this moment are saying in our inmost hearts—

"MY SOUL LOOKS BACK TO SEE
THE BURDENS THOU DIDST BEAR,
WHEN HANGING ON THE CURSED TREE,
AND HOPES HER GUILT WAS THERE."

Now, by being buried with Christ in baptism, we set our seal to the fact that the death of Christ was on our behalf, and that we were in him, and died in him, and, in token of our belief, we consent to the watery grave, and yield ourselves to be buried according to his command. This is a matter of fundamental faith—Christ dead and buried for us; in other words, substitution, suretyship, vicarious sacrifice. His death is the hinge of our confidence: we are not baptized into his example, or his life, but into his death. We hereby confess that all our salvation lies in the death of Jesus, which death we accept as having been incurred on our account.

But this is not all; because if I am to be buried, it should not be so much because I accept the substitutionary death of another for me as because I am dead myself. *Baptism is an acknowledgment of our own death in Christ.* Why should a living man be buried? Why should he even be buried because another died on his behalf? My burial with Christ means not only that he died for me, but that I died in him, so that my death with him needs a burial with him. Jesus died for us because he is one with us. The Lord Jesus Christ did not take his people's sins by an arbitrary choice of God; but it was most natural and fit and proper that he should take his people's sins, since they are his people, and he is their federal head. It behooved Christ to suffer for this reason—that he was the covenant representative of his people. He is the Head of the body, the Church; and if the members sinned, it was meet that the Head, though the Head had not sinned, should bear the consequence of the acts of the body. As there is a natural relationship between Adam and those that are in Adam, so is there between the second Adam and those that are in him. I accept what the first Adam did as my sin. Some of you may quarrel with it, and with the whole covenant dispensation, if you please; but as God has pleased to set it up, and I feel the effect of it, I see no use in my controverting it. As I accept the sin of father Adam, and feel that I sinned in him, even so with intense delight I accept the death and atoning sacrifice of my second Adam, and rejoice that in him I have died and risen again. I lived, I died, I kept the law, I satisfied justice in my covenant Head. Let me be buried in baptism that I may show to all around that I believe I was one with my Lord in his death and burial for sin.

Look at this, O child of God, and do not be afraid of it. These are Grand truths, but they are sure and comforting. You are getting among Atlantic billows now, but be not afraid. Realize the sanctifying effect of this truth. Suppose that a man had been condemned to die on account of a great crime; suppose, further, that he has actually died for that crime, and now, by some wonderful work of God, after having died he has been made to live again. He comes among men again as alive from the dead, and what ought to be the state of his mind with regard to his offence? Will he commit that crime again? A crime for which he has died? I say emphatically, God forbid. Rather should he say, "I have tasted the bitterness of this sin, and I am miraculously lifted up out of the death which it brought upon me, and made to live again: now will I hate the thing that slew me, and abhor it with all my soul." He who has received the wages of sin should learn to avoid it for the future. But you reply, "We never did die so; we were never made to suffer the due reward of our sins." Granted. But that which Christ did for you comes to the same thing, and the Lord looks upon it as the same thing. You are so one with Jesus, that you must regard his death as your death, his sufferings as the chastisement of your peace. You have died in the death of Jesus, and now by strange, mysterious grace you are brought

8

up again from the pit of corruption unto newness of life. Can you, will you, go into sin again? You have seen what God thinks of sin: you perceive that he utterly loathes it; for when it was laid on his dear Son, he did not spare him, but put him to grief and smote him to death. Can you, after that, turn back to the accursed thing which God hates? Surely, the effect of the great grief of the Saviour upon your spirit must be sanctifying. How shall we who are dead to sin live any longer therein? How shall we that have passed under its curse, and endured its awful penalty, tolerate its power? Shall we go back to this murderous, villainous, virulent, abominable evil? It cannot be. Grace forbids.

This doctrine is not the conclusion of the whole matter. The text describes us as *buried with a view to rising.* "Therefore we are buried with him by baptism unto death,"—for what object?—"that like as Christ was raised up from the dead by the glory of the Father, even so we also should walk in newness of life." Be buried in Christ! What for? That you may be dead for ever? No, but that now getting where Christ is, you may go where Christ goes. Behold him, then: he goes, first, into the sepulchre, but next out of the sepulchre; for when the third morning came he rose. If you are one with Christ at all, you must be one with him all through; you must be one with him in his death, and one with him in his burial, then you shall come to be one with him in his resurrection. Am I a dead man now? No, blessed be his name, it is written, "Because I live ye shall live also." True, I am dead in one sense, "For ye are dead"; but yet not dead in another, "For your life is hid with Christ in God"; and how is he absolutely dead who has a hidden life? No; since I am one with Christ I am what Christ is: as he is a living Christ, I am a living spirit. What a glorious thing it is to have arisen from the dead, because Christ has given us life. Our old legal life has been taken from us by the sentence of the law, and the law views us as dead; but now we have received a new life, a life out of death, resurrection-life in Christ Jesus. The life of the Christian is the life of Christ. Ours is not the life of the first creation, but of the new creation from among the dead. Now we live in newness of life, quickened unto holiness, and righteousness, and joy by the Spirit of God. The life of the flesh is a hindrance to us; our energy is in his Spirit. In the highest and best sense our life is spiritual and heavenly. This also is doctrine which is to be held most firmly.

I want you to see the force of this; for I am aiming at practical results this morning. If God has given to you and to me an entirely new life in Christ, how can that new life spend itself after the fashion of the old life? Shall the spiritual live as the carnal? How can you that were the servants of sin, but have been made free by precious blood, go back to your old slavery? When you were in the old Adam life, you lived in sin, and loved it; but now you have been dead and buried, and have come forth into newness of life: can it be that you can go back to the beggarly elements from which the Lord has brought you out? If you live in sin, you will be false to your profession, for you profess to be alive unto God? If you walk in lust, you will tread under foot the blessed doctrines of the Word of God, for these lead to holiness and purity. You would make Christianity to be a by-word and a proverb, if, after all, you who were quickened from your spiritual death should exhibit a conduct no better than the life of ordinary men, and little superior to what your former life used to be. As many of you as have been baptized have said to the world,—We are dead to the world, and we have come forth into a new life. Our fleshly desires are henceforth to be viewed as dead, for now we live after a fresh order of things. The Holy Spirit has wrought in us a new nature, and though we are in the world, we are not of it, but are new-made men, "created anew in Christ Jesus." This is the doctrine which we avow to all mankind, that Christ died and rose again, and that his people died and rose again in him. Out of the doctrine grows death unto sin and life unto God, and we wish by every action and every movement of our lives to teach it to all who see us.

So far the doctrine: is it not a precious one indeed? Oh, if you be indeed one with Christ, shall the world find you polluting yourselves? Shall the members of a generous, gracious Head be covetous and grasping? Shall the members of a glorious, pure, and perfect Head be defiled with the lusts of the flesh and the follies of a vain life? If believers are indeed so identified with Christ that they are his fullness, should they not be holiness itself? If we live by virtue of our union with his body, how can we live as other Gentiles do? How is it that so many professors exhibit a mere worldly life, living for business and for pleasure, but not for God, in God, or with God? They sprinkle a little religion on a worldly life, and so hope to Christianize it. But it will not do. I am bound to live as Christ would have lived under my circumstances; in my private chamber or in my public pulpit, I am bound to be what Christ would have been in like case. I am bound to prove to men that union to Christ is no fiction, or fanatical sentiment: but that we are swayed by the same principles and actuated by the same motives.

Baptism is thus an embodied creed, and you may read it in these words: "Buried with him in baptism, wherein also ye are risen with him through the faith of the operation of God, who hath raised him from the dead."

II. But, secondly, A REALIZED UNION WITH CHRIST is also set forth in baptism, and this is rather a matter of experience than of doctrine.

1. First, there is, as a matter of actual experience in the true believer, *death*. "Know ye not that so many of us as were baptized into Jesus Christ were baptized into his death?" It must be contrary to all law to bury those who are yet alive. Until they are dead, men can have no right to be buried. Very well, then, the Christian is dead,—dead, first, *to the dominion of sin*. Whenever sin called him aforetime he answered, "Here am I, for thou didst call me." Sin ruled his members, and if sin said, "Do this," he did it, like the soldiers obedient to their centurion; for sin ruled over all the parts of his nature, and exercised over him a supreme tyranny. Grace has changed all this. When we are converted we become dead to the dominion of sin. If sin calls us now, we refuse to come, for we are dead. If sin commands us we will not obey, for we are dead to its authority. Sin comes to us now—oh, that it did not,—and it finds in us the old corruption which is crucified, but not yet dead; but it has no dominion over our true life. Blessed be God, sin cannot reign over us, though it may assail us and work us harm. "Sin shall not have dominion over you; for ye are not under law, but under grace." We sin, but not with allowance. With what grief we look back upon our transgressions! How earnestly do we endeavour to avoid them! Sin tries to maintain its usurped power over us; but we do not acknowledge it as our sovereign. Evil enters us now as an interloper and a stranger, and works sad havoc, but it does not abide in us upon the throne; it is an alien, and despised, and no more honoured and delighted in. We are dead to the reigning power of sin.

The believer, if spiritually buried with Christ, is *dead to the desire of any such power*. "What!" say you, "do not godly men have sinful desires?" Alas, they do. The old nature that is in them lusteth towards sin; but the true man, the real *ego*, desires to be purged of every speck or trace of evil. The law in the members would fain urge to sin, but the life in the heart constrains to holiness. I can honestly say, for my own self, that the deepest desire of my soul is to live a perfect life. If I could have my own best desire, I would never sin again; and though, alas, I do consent to sin so that I become responsible when I transgress, yet my innermost self loathes iniquity. Sin is my bondage, not my pleasure; my misery, not my delight; at the thought of it I cry out, "O wretched man that I am! who shall deliver me?" In our heart of hearts our spirit cleaves steadfastly to that which is good, and true, and heavenly, so that the real man delights in the law of

God, and follows hard after goodness. The main current and true bent of our soul's wish and will is not towards sin, and the apostle taught us no mere fancy when he said, "For he that is dead is freed from sin."

Moreover, in the next place we are dead *as to the pursuits and aims of the sinning and ungodly life*. Brethren, are any of you that profess to be God's servants living for yourselves? Then you are not God's servants; for he that is really born again lives unto God: the object of his life is the glory of God and the good of his fellow-men. This is the prize that is set before the quickened man, and towards this he runs. "I do not run that way," says one. Very well, then you will not come to the desired end. If you are running after the pleasures of the world or the riches of it, you may win the prize you run for, but you cannot win "the prize of our high calling in Christ Jesus." I hope that many of us can honestly say that we are now dead to every object in life, except the glory of God in Christ Jesus. We are in the world, and have to live as other men do, carrying on our ordinary business; but all this is subordinate, and held in as with bit and bridle; our aims are above yon changeful moon. The flight of our soul, like that of an eagle, is above these clouds: though that bird of the sun alights upon the rock, or even descends to the plain, yet its joy is to dwell above, out soaring the lightning, rising over the black head of the tempest, and looking down upon all earthly things. Henceforth our grace-given life speeds onward and upward; we are not of the world, and the world's engagements are not those upon which we spend our noblest powers.

Again, we are dead in this sense, that we are dead *to the guidance of sin*. The lust of the flesh drives a man this way and that way. He steers his course by the question, "What is most pleasant? What will give me most present gratification?" The way of the ungodly is mapped out by the hand of selfish desire: but you that are true Christians have another guide, you are led by the Spirit in a right way. You ask, "What is good and what is acceptable in the sight of the Most High?" Your daily prayer is, "Lord, show me what thou wouldest have me to do?" You are alive to the teachings of the Spirit, who will lead you into all truth; but you are deaf, yea, dead to the dogmas of carnal wisdom, the oppositions of philosophy, the errors of proud human wisdom. Blind guides who fall with their victims into the ditch are shunned by you, for you have chosen the way of the Lord. What a blessed state of heart this is! I trust, my brethren, that we have fully realized it! We know the Shepherd's voice, and a stranger we will not follow. One is our teacher, and we submit our understandings to his infallible instruction.

Our text must have had a very forcible meaning among the Romans in Paul's time, for they were sunk in all manner of odious vices. Take an average Roman of that period, and you would have found in him a man accustomed to spend a large part of his time in the amphitheater, hardened by the brutal sight of bloody shows, in which gladiators slew each other to amuse a holiday crowd. Taught in such a school, the Roman was cruel to the last degree, and withal ferocious in the indulgence of his passions. A depraved man was not regarded as being at all degraded; not only nobles and emperors were monsters of vice, but the public teachers were impure. When those who were regarded as moral were corrupt, you may imagine what the immoral were. "Enjoy yourself; follow after the pleasures of the flesh," was the rule of the age. Christianity was the introduction of a new element. See here a Roman converted by the grace of God! What a change is in him! His neighbours say, "You were not at the amphitheater this morning. How could you miss the sight of the hundred Germans who tore out each other's bowels?" "No," he says, "I was not there; I could not bear to be there. I am totally dead to it. If you were to force me to be there, I must shut my eyes, for I could not look on murder committed in sport!" The Christian did not resort to places of licentiousness; he was as good as dead to such filthiness. The fashions and customs of the age were such that Christians could not consent to them, and so they became dead to society. It was not merely that Christians did not go into open sin, but they spoke of it with horror, and their lives rebuked it. Things which the multitude counted a joy, and talked of exultingly, gave no comfort to the follower of Jesus, for he was dead to such evils. This is our solemn avowal when we come forward to be baptized. We say by acts which are louder than words that we are dead to those things in which sinners take delight, and we wish to be so accounted.

2. The next thought in baptism is *burial*. Death comes first, and burial follows. Now, what is burial, brethren? Burial is, first of all, *the seal of death*; it is the certificate of decease. "Is such a man dead?" say you. Another answers, "Why, dear sir, he was buried a year ago." There have been instances of persons being buried alive, and I am afraid that the thing happens with sad frequency in baptism, but it is unnatural, and by no means the rule. I fear that many have been buried alive in baptism, and have therefore risen and walked out of the grave just as they were. But if burial is true, it is a certificate of death. If I am able to say in very truth, "I was buried with Christ thirty years ago," I must surely be dead. Certainly the world thought so, for not long after my burial with Jesus I began to preach

his name, and by that time the world thought me very far gone, and said, "He stinketh." They began to say all manner of evil against the preacher; but the more I stank in their nostrils the better I liked it, for the surer I was that I was really dead to the world. It is good for a Christian to be offensive to wicked men. See how our Master stank in the esteem of the godless when they cried, "Away with him, away with him!" Though no corruption could come near his blessed body, yet his perfect character was not savoured by that perverse generation. There must, then, be in us death to the world, and some of the effects of death, or our baptism is void. As burial is the certificate of death, so is burial with Christ the seal of our mortification to the world.

But burial is, next, *the displaying of death*. While the man is indoors the passers-by do not know that he is dead; but when the funeral takes place, and he is carried through the streets, everybody knows that he is dead. This is what baptism ought to be. The believer's death to sin is at first a secret, but by an open confession he bids all men know that he is dead with Christ. Baptism is the funeral rite by which death to sin is openly set forth before all men.

Next, burial is *the separateness of death*. The dead man no longer remains in the house, but is placed apart as one who ceases to be numbered with the living. A corpse is not welcome company. Even the most beloved object after a while cannot be tolerated when death has done his work upon it. Even Abraham, who had been so long united with his beloved Sarah, is heard to say, "Bury my dead out of my sight." Such is the believer when his death to the world is fully known: he is poor company for worldlings, and they shun him as a damper upon their revelry. The true saint is put into the separated class with Christ, according to his word, "If they have persecuted me, they will also persecute you." The saint is put away in the same grave as his Lord; for as he was, so are we also in this world. He is shut up by the world in the one cemetery of the faithful, if I may so call it, where all that are in Christ are dead to the world together, with this epitaph for them all, "And ye are dead, and your life is hid with Christ in God."

And the grave is the place—I do not know where to get a word—*of the settledness of death*; for when a man is dead and buried you never expect to see him come home again: so far as this world is concerned, death and burial are irrevocable. They tell me that spirits walk the earth, and we have all read in the newspaper "The Truth about Ghosts," but I have my doubts on the subject. In spiritual things, however, I am afraid that some are not so buried with Christ but what they walk a great deal among the tombs. I am grieved at heart that it should be so. The man in Christ cannot walk as a ghost, because he is alive somewhere else; he has received a new being, and therefore he cannot mutter and peep among the dead hypocrites around him. See what our chapter saith about our Lord: "Christ being raised from the dead dieth no more: death hath no more dominion over him. For in that he died, he died unto sin once: but in that he liveth, he liveth unto God." If we have been once raised from dead works we shall never go back to them again. I may sin, but sin can never have dominion over me; I may be a transgressor and wander much from my God, but never can I go back to the old death again. When my Lord's grace got hold of me, and buried me, he wrought in my soul the conviction that henceforth and for ever I was to the world a dead man. I am right glad that I made no compromise, but came right out. I have drawn the sword, and thrown away the scabbard. Tell the world they need not try to fetch us back, for we are spoiled for them as much as if we were dead. All they could have would be our carcasses. Tell the world not to tempt us any longer, for our hearts are changed. Sin may charm the old man who hangs there upon the cross, and he may turn his leering eye that way, but he cannot follow up his glance, for he cannot get down from the cross: the Lord has taken care to use the mallet well, and he has fastened his hands and feet right firmly, so that the crucified flesh must still remain in the place of doom and death. Yet the true, the genuine life within us cannot die, for it is born of God; neither can it abide in the tombs, for its call is to purity and joy and liberty; and to that call it yields itself.

3. We have come as far as death and burial; but baptism, according to the text, represents also *resurrection*: "That like as Christ was raised up from the dead by the glory of the Father, even so we also should walk in newness of life." Now, notice that the man who is dead in Christ, and buried in Christ, is also raised in Christ, and this is a *special work upon him*. All the dead are not raised, but our Lord himself is "the firstfruits of them that slept." He is the first-begotten from among the dead. Resurrection was a special work upon the body of Christ by which he was raised up, and that work, begun upon the Head, will continue till all the members partake of it, for—

"THOUGH OUR INBRED SINS REQUIRE
OUR FLESH TO SEE THE DUST;

YET AS THE LORD OUR SAVIOUR ROSE, SO ALL HIS FOLLOWERS MUST."

As to our soul and spirit, the resurrection has begun upon us. It has not come to our bodies yet, but it will be given to them at the appointed day. For the present a special work has been wrought upon us by which we have been raised up from among the dead. Brethren, if you had been dead and buried, and had been lying one night, say, in Woking Cemetery, and if a divine voice had called you right up from the grave when the silent stars were shining on the open heath—if, I say, you had risen right out from the green mound of turf, what a lonely being you would have been in the vast cemetery amid the stilly night! How you would sit down on the grave and wait for morning! That is very much your condition with regard to the present evil world. You were once like the rest of the sinners around you, dead in sin, and sleeping in the grave of evil custom. The Lord by his power has called you out of your grave, and now you are alive in the midst of death. There can be no fellowship here for you; for what communion have the living with the dead? The man out there in the cemetery just quickened would find none among all the dead around him with whom he could converse, and you can find no companions in this world. There lies a skull, but it sees not from the eyeholes; neither is there speech in its grim mouth. I see a mass of bones lying in yon corner: the living one looks at them, but they cannot hear or speak. Imagine yourself there. All that you would say to the bones would be to ask, "Can these dry bones live?" You would be a foreigner in that home of corruption, and you would haste to get away. That is your condition in the world: God has raised you up from among the dead, from out of the company among whom you had your former conversation. Now, I pray you, do not go and scratch into the earth, to tear up the graves to find a friend there. Who would rend open a coffin and cry, "Come, you must drink with me! You must go to the theatre with me"? No, we dread the idea of association with the dead, and I tremble when I see a professor trying to have communion with worldly men. "Come ye out from among them; be ye separate; touch not the unclean thing." You know what would happen to you if you were thus raised, and were forced to sit close to a dead body newly taken from the grave. You would cry, "I cannot bear it; I cannot endure it"; you would get to the wind side of the horrid corpse. So with a man that is really alive unto God: deeds of injustice, oppression, or unchastity he cannot endure; for life loaths corruption.

Notice that, as we are raised up by a special work from among the dead, that rising is *by divine power*. Christ is brought again "from the dead by the glory of the Father." What means that? Why did it not say, "by the power of the Father"? Ah, beloved, glory is a grander word; for all the attributes of God are displayed in all their solemn pomp in the raising of Christ from the dead. There was the Lord's faithfulness; for had he not declared that his soul should not rest in hell, neither should His Holy One see corruption? Was not the love of the Father seen there? I am sure it was a delight to the heart of God to bring back life to the body of his dear Son. And so, when you and I are raised out of our death in sin, it is not merely God's power, it is not merely God's wisdom that is seen, it is "the glory of the Father." Oh, to think that every child of God that has been quickened has been quickened by "the glory of the Father. " It has taken not alone the Holy Spirit, and the work of Jesus, and the work of the Father, but the very "glory of the Father." If the tiniest spark of spiritual life has to be created by "the glory of the Father," what will be the glory of that life when it comes into its full perfection, and we shall be like Christ, and see him as he is! O beloved, value highly the new life which God has given you. Think of it as making you richer than if you had a sea of pearls, greater than if you were descended from the loftiest of princes. There is in you that which it required all the attributes of God to create. He could make a world by power alone, but you must be raised from the dead by "the glory of the Father."

Notice next, that this life *is entirely new*. We are to "walk in newness of life." The life of a Christian is an entirely different thing from the life of other men, entirely different from his own life before his conversion, and when people try to counterfeit it, they cannot accomplish the task. A person writes you a letter and wants to make you think he is a believer, but within about half-a-dozen sentences there occurs a line which betrays the imposter. The hypocrite has very neatly copied our expressions, but not quite. There is a freemasonry among us, and the outside world watch us a bit, and by-and-by they pick up certain of our signs; but there is a private sign which they can never imitate, and therefore at a certain point they break down. A godless man may pray as much as a Christian, read as much of the Bible as a Christian, and even go beyond us in externals; but there is a secret which he knows not and cannot counterfeit. The life divine is so totally new that the unconverted have no copy to work by. In every Christian it is as new as if he were the very first Christian. Even though in every one it is the image and superscription of Christ, yet there is a milled edge or a something about the real silver that these counterfeits cannot get a hold of. It is a new, a novel, a fresh, a divine thing.

And, lastly, this life *is an active thing*. I have often wished that Paul had not been so fast when I have been reading him. His style travels in seven-leagued boots. He does not write like an ordinary man. I beg to tell him that if he had written this text according to proper order, it should run, "Like as Christ was raised up from the dead by the glory of the Father, even so we also should be raised from the dead." But see; Paul has got over ever so much ground while we are talking: he has reached to "walking." The walking includes the living, of which it is the sign, and Paul thinks so fast when the Spirit of God is upon him that he has passed beyond the cause to the effect. No sooner do we get the new life than we become active: we do not sit down and say, "I have received a new life: how grateful I ought to be. I will quietly enjoy myself." Oh dear, no. We have something to do directly we are alive, and we begin walking, and so the Lord keeps us all our lives in his work; he does not allow us to sit down contented with the mere fact that we live, nor does he allow us to spend all our time in examining whether we are alive or no; but he gives us one battle to fight, and then another; he gives us his house to build, his farm to till, his children to nurse, and his sheep to feed. At times we have fierce struggles with our own spirit, and fears lest sin and Satan should prevail, till our life is scarce discerned by itself, but it is always discerned by its acts. The life that is given to those who were dead with Christ is an energetic, forceful life, that is evermore busy for Christ, and would, if it could, move heaven and earth and subdue all things unto him who is its Head.

This life Paul tells us is *an unending one*. Once get it, and it will never go from you. "Christ being raised from the dead dieth no more."

Next, it is a life which is *not under the law or under sin*. Christ came under the law when he was here, and he had our sin laid on him, and therefore died; but after he rose again there was no sin laid on him. In his resurrection both the sinner and the Surety are free. What had Christ to do after his rising? To bear any more sin? No, but just to live unto God. That is where you and I are. We have no sin to carry now; it was all laid on Christ. What have we to do? Every time we have the headache, or feel ill, are we to cry out, "This is a punishment for my sin"? Nothing of the kind. Our punishment is all done with, for we have borne the capital sentence, and are dead: our new life must be unto God.

18

"ALL THAT REMAINS FOR ME
IS BUT TO LOVE AND SING,
AND WAIT UNTIL THE ANGELS COME
TO BEAR ME TO THE KING."

I have now to serve him and delight myself in him, and use the power which he gives me of calling others from the dead, saying, "Awake, thou that sleepest, and arise from the dead, and Christ shall give thee light." I am not going back to the grave of spiritual death nor to my grave-clothes of sin; but by divine grace I will still believe in Jesus, and go from strength to strength, not under law, not fearing hell, nor hoping to merit heaven, but as a new creature, loving because loved, living for Christ because Christ lives in me, rejoicing in glorious hope of that which is yet to be revealed by virtue of my oneness in Christ.

Poor sinner, you do not know anything about this death and burial, and you never will till you have power to become sons of God, and that he gives to as many as believe on his name. Believe on his name, and it is all yours. Amen and Amen.

2

Baptismal Regeneration

June 5, 1864
Metropolitan Tabernacle, Newington

"And he said unto them, Go ye into all the world, and preach the gospel to every creature. He that believeth and is baptized shall be saved; but he that believeth not shall be damned."

—Mark 16:15-16

IN THE PRECEDING VERSE OUR Lord Jesus Christ gives us some little insight into the natural character of the apostles whom he selected to be the first ministers of the Word. They were evidently men of like passions with us, and needed to be rebuked even as we do. On the occasion when our Lord sent forth the eleven to preach the gospel to every creature, he "appeared unto them as they sat at meat, and upbraided them with their unbelief and hardness of heart, because they believed not them which had seen him after he was risen;" from which we may surely gather that to preach the Word, the Lord was pleased to choose imperfect men; men, too, who of themselves were very weak in the grace of faith in which it was most important that they should excel. Faith is the conquering grace, and is of all things the main requisite in the preacher of the Word; and yet the honoured men who were chosen to be the leaders of the divine crusade needed a rebuke concerning their unbelief. Why was this? Why, my brethren, because the Lord has ordained evermore that we should have this treasure in *earthen* vessels, that the excellency of the power may be of God and not of us. If you should find a perfect minister, then might the praise and honour of his usefulness accrue to man; but God is frequently pleased to select for eminent usefulness men evidently honest and sincere, but who have some manifest infirmity by which all the glory is cast off from them and laid upon Himself, and upon Himself alone. Let it never be supposed that we who are God's ministers either excuse our faults or pretend to perfection. We labour to walk in holiness, but we cannot claim to be all that we wish to be. We do not base the claims of God's truth upon the spotlessness of our characters, but upon the fact that it comes from him. You have believed in spite of our infirmities, and not because of our virtues; if, indeed, you had believed our word because of our supposed perfection, your faith would stand in the excellency of man and not in the power of God. We come unto you often with much trembling, sorrowing over our follies and weaknesses, but we deliver to you God's Word as God's Word, and we beseech you to receive it not as coming from us poor, sinful mortals, but as proceeding from the Eternal and Thrice Holy God; and if you so receive it, and by its own vital force are moved and stirred up towards God and his ways, then is the work of the Word sure work, which it could not and would not be if it rested in any way upon man.

Our Lord having thus given us an insight into the character of the persons whom he has chosen to proclaim his truth, then goes on to deliver to the chosen champions, their commission for the Holy War. I pray you mark the words with solemn care. He sums up in a few words the whole of their work, and at the same time foretells the result of it, telling them that some would doubtless believe and so be saved, and some on the other hand would not believe and would most certainly, therefore, be damned, that is, condemned for ever to the penalties of God's wrath. The lines containing the commission of our ascended Lord are certainly of the utmost importance, and demand devout attention and implicit obedience, not only from all who aspire to the work of the ministry, but also from all who hear the message of mercy. A clear understanding of these words is absolutely necessary to our success in our Master's work, for if we do not understand the commission it is not at all likely that we shall discharge it aright. To alter these words were more than impertinence, it would involve the crime of treason against the authority of Christ and the best interests of the souls of men. O for grace to be very jealous here.

Wherever the apostles went they met with obstacles to the preaching of the gospel, and the more open and effectual was the door of utterance the more numerous were the adversaries. These brave men who wielded the sword of the Spirit as to put to flight all their foes; and this they did not by craft and guile, but by making a direct cut at the error which impeded them. Never did they dream for a moment of adapting the gospel to the unhallowed tastes or prejudices of the people, but at once directly and boldly they brought down with both their hands the mighty sword of the Spirit upon the crown of the opposing error. This morning, in the name of the Lord of Hosts, my Helper and Defense, I shall attempt to do the same; and if I should provoke some hostility—if I should through speaking what I believe to be the truth lose the friendship of some and stir up the enmity of more, I cannot help it. The burden of the Lord is upon me, and I must deliver my soul. I have been loath enough to undertake the work, but I am forced to it by an awful and overwhelming sense of solemn duty. As I am soon to appear before my Master's bar, I will this day, if ever in my life, bear my testimony for truth, and run all risks. I am content to be cast out as evil if it must be so, but I cannot, I dare not, hold my peace. The Lord knoweth I have nothing in my heart but the purest love to the souls of those whom I feel imperatively called to rebuke sternly in the Lord's name. Among my hearers and readers, a considerable number will censure if not condemn me, but I cannot help it. If I forfeit your love for truth's sake I am grieved for you, but I cannot, I dare not, do otherwise. It is as much as my soul is worth to hold my peace any longer, and whether you approve or not I must speak out. Did I ever court your approbation? It is sweet to everyone to be applauded; but if for the sake of the comforts of respectability and the smiles of men any Christian minister shall keep back a part of his testimony, his Master at the last shall require it at his hands. This day, standing in the immediate presence of God, I shall speak honestly what I feel, as the Holy Spirit shall enable me; and I shall leave the matter with you to judge concerning it, as you will answer for that judgment at the last great day.

I find that the great error which we have to contend with throughout England (and it is growing more and more), is one in direct opposition to my text, well known to you as the doctrine of baptismal regeneration. We will confront this dogma with the assertion, that BAPTISM WITHOUT FAITH SAVES NO ONE. The text says, "He *that believeth* and is baptized shall be saved;" but whether a man be baptized or no, it asserts that *"he that believeth not* shall be damned:" so that baptism does not save the unbeliever, nay, it does not in any degree exempt him from the common doom of all the ungodly. He may have baptism, or he may not have baptism, but if he believeth not, he shall be in any case most surely damned. Let him be baptized by immersion or sprinkling, in his infancy, or in his adult age, if he be not led to put his trust in Jesus Christ—if he remaineth an unbeliever, then this terrible doom is pronounced upon him—"He that believeth not shall be damned." I am not aware that any Protestant Church in England teaches the doctrine of baptismal regeneration except one, and that happens to be the corporation which with none too much humility calls itself *the* Church of England. This very powerful sect does not teach this doctrine merely through a section of its ministers, who might charitably be considered as evil branches of the vine, but it openly, boldly, and plainly declares this doctrine in her own appointed standard, the Book of Common Prayer, and that in words so express, that while language is the channel of conveying intelligible sense, no process short of violent wresting from their plain meaning can ever make them say anything else.

Here are the words: we quote them from the Catechism which is intended for the instruction of youth, and is naturally very plain and simple, since it would be foolish to trouble the young with metaphysical refinements. The child is asked its name, and then questioned, "Who gave you this name?" *"My godfathers and godmothers in my baptism; wherein I was made a member of Christ, the child of God, and an inheritor of the kingdom of heaven."* Is not this definite and plain enough? I prize the words for their candour; they could not speak more plainly. Three times over the thing is put, lest there should be any doubt in it. The word *regeneration* may, by some sort of juggling, be made to mean something else, but here there can be no misunderstanding. The child is not only made "a member of Christ"—union to Jesus is no mean spiritual gift—but he is made in baptism "the child of God" also; and, since the rule is, "if children then heirs," he is also made "an inheritor of the kingdom of heaven." Nothing can be more plain. I venture to say that while honesty remains on earth the meaning of these words will not admit of dispute. It is clear as noon day that, as the Rubric hath it, "Fathers, mothers, masters, and dames, are to cause their children, servants, and apprentices," no matter how idle, giddy, or wicked they may be, to learn the Catechism, and to say that in baptism they were made members of Christ and children of God. The form for the administration of this baptism is scarcely less plain and outspoken, seeing that thanks are expressly returned unto Almighty God, because the person baptized is regenerate. *"Then shall the priest say, 'Seeing now, dearly beloved brethren, that this child is regenerate and grafted into the body of Christ's Church, let us give thanks unto Almighty God for these benefits; and with one accord make our prayers unto him, that this child may lead the rest of his life according to this beginning.'"* Nor is this all, for to leave no mistake, we have the words of the thanksgiving prescribed, *"Then shall the priest say, 'We yield thee hearty thanks, most merciful Father, that it hath pleased thee to regenerate this infant with thy Holy Spirit, to receive him for thine own child by adoption, and to incorporate him into thy holy Church.'"*

This, then, is the clear and unmistakable teaching of a Church calling itself Protestant. I am not now dealing at all with the question of infant baptism: I have nothing to do with that this morning. I am now considering the question of baptismal regeneration, whether in adults or infants, or ascribed to sprinkling, pouring, or immersion. Here is a Church which teaches every Lord's day in the Sunday-school, and should, according to the Rubric, teach openly in the Church, all children that they were made members of Christ, children of God, and inheritors of the kingdom of heaven when they were baptized! Here is a professedly Protestant Church, which, every time its minister goes to the font, declares that every person there receiving baptism is there and then "regenerated and grafted into the body of Christ's Church."

"But," I hear many good people exclaim, "there are many good clergymen in the Church who do not believe in baptismal regeneration." To this my answer is prompt. Why then do they belong to a Church which teaches that doctrine in the plainest terms? I am told that many in the Church of England preach against her own teaching. I know they do, and herein I rejoice in their enlightenment, but I question, gravely question their morality. To take oath that I sincerely assent and consent to a doctrine which I do not believe, would to my conscience appear little short of perjury, if not absolute downright perjury; but those who do so must be judged by their own Lord. For me to take money for defending what I do not believe—for me to take the money of a Church, and then to preach against what are most evidently its doctrines—I say *for me* to do this (I judge others as I would that they should judge me) for me, or for any other simple, honest man to do so, were an atrocity so great, that if I had perpetrated the deed, I should consider myself out of the pale of truthfulness, honesty, and common morality. Sirs, when I accepted the office of minister of this congregation, I looked to see what were your articles of faith; if I had not believed them I should not have accepted your call, and when I change my opinions, rest assured that as an honest man I shall resign the office, for how could I profess one thing in your declaration of faith, and quite another thing in my own preaching? Would I accept your pay, and then stand up every Sabbath-day and talk against the doctrines of your standards? For clergymen to swear or say that they give their solemn assent and consent to what they do not believe is one of the grossest pieces of immorality perpetrated in England, and is most pestilential in its influence, since it directly teaches men to lie whenever it seems necessary to do so in order to get a living or increase their supposed usefulness: it is in fact an open testimony from priestly lips that at least in ecclesiastical matters falsehood may express truth, and truth itself is a mere unimportant nonentity. I know of nothing more calculated to debauch the public mind than a want of straightforwardness in ministers; and when worldly men hear ministers denouncing the very things which their own Prayer Book teaches, they imagine that words have no meaning among ecclesiastics, and that vital differences in religion are merely a matter of *tweedle-dee* and *tweedle-dum*, and that it does not much matter what a man does believe so long as he is charitable towards other people. If baptism does regenerate people, let the fact be preached with a trumpet tongue, and let no man be ashamed of his belief in it. If this be really their creed, by all means let them have full liberty for its propagation. My brethren, those are honest Churchmen in this matter who, subscribing to the Prayer Book, believe in baptismal regeneration, and preach it plainly. God forbid that we should censure those who believe that baptism saves the soul, because they adhere to a Church which teaches the same doctrine. So far they are honest men; and in England, where else, let them never lack a full toleration. Let us oppose their teaching by all Scriptural and intelligent means, but let us respect their courage in plainly giving us their views. I hate their doctrine, but I love their honesty; and as they speak but what they believe to be true, let them speak it out, and the more clearly the better. Out with it, sirs, be it what it may, but do let us know what you mean. For my part, I love to stand foot to foot with an honest foeman. To open warfare, bold and true hearts raise no objection but the ground of quarrel; it is covert enmity which we have most cause to fear, and best reason to loathe. That crafty kindness which inveigles me to sacrifice principle is the serpent in the grass—deadly to the incautious wayfarer. Where union and friendship are not cemented by truth, they are an unhallowed confederacy. It is time that there should be an end put to the flirtations of honest men with those who believe one way and swear another. If men believe baptism works regeneration, let them say so; but if they do not so believe it in their hearts, and yet subscribe, and yet more, get their livings by subscribing to words asserting it, let them find congenial associates among men who can equivocate and shuffle, for honest men will neither ask nor accept their friendship.

We ourselves are not dubious on this point, we protest that persons are not saved by being baptized. In such an audience as this, I am almost ashamed to go into the matter, because you surely know better than to be misled. Nevertheless, for the good of others we will drive at it. We hold that persons are not saved by baptism, for we think, first of all that *it seems out of character with the spiritual religion which Christ came to teach,* that he should make salvation depend upon mere ceremony. Judaism might possibly absorb the ceremony by way of type into her ordinances essential to eternal life; for it was religion of types and shadows. The false religions of the heathen might inculcate salvation by a physical process, but Jesus

Christ claims for his faith that it is purely spiritual, and how could he connect regeneration with a peculiar application of aqueous fluid? I cannot see how it would be a spiritual gospel, but I can see how it would be mechanical, if I were sent forth to teach that the mere dropping of so many drops upon the brow, or even the plunging a person in water could save the soul. This seems to me to be the most mechanical religion now existing, and to be on a par with the praying windmills of Thibet, or the climbing up and down of Pilate's staircase to which Luther subjected himself in the days of his darkness. The operation of water-baptism does not appear even to my faith to touch the point involved in the regeneration of the soul. What is the necessary connection between water and the overcoming of sin? I cannot see any connection which can exist between sprinkling, or immersion, and regeneration, so that the one shall necessarily be tied to the other in the absence of faith. Used by faith, had God commanded it, miracles might be wrought; but without faith or even consciousness, as in the case of babes, how can spiritual benefits be connected necessarily with the sprinkling of water? If this be your teaching, that regeneration goes with baptism, I say it looks like the teaching of a spurious Church, which has craftily invented a mechanical salvation to deceive ignorant, sensual, and grovelling minds, rather than the teaching of the most profoundly spiritual of all teachers, who rebuked Scribes and Pharisees for regarding outward rites as more important than inward grace.

But it strikes me that a more forcible argument is that *the dogma is not supported by facts*. Are all persons who are baptized children of God? Well, let us look at the divine family. Let us mark their resemblance to their glorious Parent! Am I untruthful if I say that thousands of those who were baptized in their infancy are now in our goals? You can ascertain the fact if you please, by application to prison authorities. Do you believe that these men, many of whom have been living by plunder, felony, burglary, or forgery, are regenerate? If so, the Lord deliver us from such regeneration. Are these villains members of Christ? If so, Christ has sadly altered since the day when he was holy, harmless, undefiled, separate from sinners. Has he really taken baptized drunkards and harlots to be members of his body? Do you not revolt at the supposition? It is a well-known fact that baptized persons have been hanged. Surely it can hardly be right to hang the inheritors of the kingdom of heaven! Our sheriffs have much to answer for when they officiate at the execution of the children of God, and suspend the members of Christ on the gallows! What a detestable farce is that which is transacted at the open grave, when "a dear brother" who has died drunk is buried in a "sure and certain hope of the resurrection of eternal life," and the prayer that "when we shall depart this life we may rest in Christ, as our hope is that this our brother doth." Here is a regenerate brother, who having defiled the village by constant uncleanness and bestial drunkenness, died without a sign of repentance, and yet the professed minister of God solemnly accords him funeral rites which are denied to unbaptized innocents, and puts the reprobate into the earth in "sure and certain hope of the resurrection to eternal life." If old Rome in her worst days ever perpetrated a grosser piece of imposture than this, I do not read things aright; if it does not require a Luther to cry down this hypocrisy as much as Popery ever did, then I do not even know that twice two make four. Do we find—we who baptize on profession of faith, and baptize by immersion in a way which is confessed to be correct, though not allowed by some to be absolutely necessary to its validity—do we who baptize in the name of the sacred Trinity as others do, do we find that baptism regenerates? *We do not.* Neither in the righteous nor the wicked do we find regeneration wrought by baptism. We have never met with one believer, however instructed in divine things, who could trace his regeneration to his baptism; and on the other hand, we confess it with sorrow, but still with no surprise, that we have seen those whom we have ourselves baptized, according to apostolic precedent, go back into the world and wander into the foulest sin, and their baptism has scarcely been so much as a restraint to them, because they have not believed in the Lord Jesus Christ. Facts all show that whatever good there may be in baptism, it certainly does not make a man "a member of Christ, the child of God, and an inheritor of the kingdom of heaven," or else many thieves, whoremongers, drunkards, fornicators, and murderers, are members of Christ, the children of God, and inheritors of the kingdom of heaven. Facts, brethren, are against this Popish doctrine; and facts are stubborn things.

Yet further, I am persuaded *that the performance styled baptism by the Prayer Book is not at all likely to regenerate and save.* How is the thing done? One is very curious to know when one hears of an operation which makes men members of Christ, children of God, and inheritors of the kingdom of heaven, how the thing is done. It must in itself be a holy thing truthful in all its details, and edifying in every portion. Now, we will suppose we have a company gathered round the water, be it more or less, and the process of regeneration is about to be performed. We will suppose them all to be *godly people*. The clergyman officiating is a profound believer in the Lord Jesus, and the father and mother are exemplary Christians, and the godfathers and godmothers are all gracious persons. We will suppose this—it is a supposition fraught with charity, but it may be correct. What are these godly people supposed to say? Let us look to the Prayer Book. The clergyman is suppose to tell these people, *"Ye have heard also that our Lord Jesus Christ hath promised in his gospel to grant all these things that ye have prayed for: which promise he, for his part, will most surely keep and perform. Wherefore, after this promise made by Christ, this infant must also faithfully, for his part, promise by you that are his sureties (until he come of age to take it upon himself) that he will renounce the devil and all his works, and constantly believe God's holy Word, and obediently keep his commandments."* This small child is to promise to do this, or more truly others are to take upon themselves to promise, and even *vow* that he shall do so. But we must not break the quotation, and therefore let us return to the Book. "I demand therefore, dost thou, in the name of this child, renounce the devil and all his works, the vain pomp and glory of the world, with all covetous desires of the same, and the carnal desires of the flesh, so that thou wilt not follow, nor be led by them?" Answers "I renounce them all." That is to say, on the name and behalf of this tender infant about to be baptized, these godly people, these enlightened Christian people, these who know better, who are not dupes, who know all the while that they are promising impossibilities—renounce on behalf of this child what they find it very hard to renounce for themselves—"all covetous desires of the world and the carnal desires of the flesh, so that they will not follow nor be led by them." How can they harden their faces to utter such a false promise, such a mockery of renunciation before the presence of the Father Almighty? Might not angels weep as they hear the awful promise uttered? Then in the presence of high heaven they profess on behalf of this child that he steadfastly believes the creed, when they know, or might pretty shrewdly judge that the little creature is not yet a steadfast believer in anything, much less in Christ's going down into hell. Mark, they do not say merely that the babe *shall* believe the creed, but they affirm that he does, for they answer in the child's name, "All this I steadfastly believe. Not *we* steadfastly believe," but *I*, the little baby there, unconscious of all their professions and confessions of faith. In answer to the question, "Wilt thou be baptized in this faith?" they reply for the infant, "That is my desire." Surely the infant has no desire in the matter, or at the least, no one has been authorized to declare any desires on his behalf. But this is not all, for then these godly, intelligent people next promise on the behalf of the infant, that "he shall obediently keep all God's holy will and commandments, and walk in the same all the days of his life." Now, I ask you, dear friends, you who know what true religion means, can you walk in all God's holy commandments yourselves? Dare you make this day a vow on your own part, that you would renounce the devil and all his works, the pomps and vanities of this wicked world, and all the sinful lusts of the flesh? Dare you, before God, make such a promise as that? You desire such holiness, you earnestly strive after it, but you look for it from God's promise, not from your own. If you dare make such vows I doubt your knowledge of your own hearts and of the spirituality of Gods's law. But even if you could do this for yourself, would you venture to make such a promise for any other person? For the best-born infant on earth? Come, brethren, what say you? Is not your reply ready and plain? There is not room for two opinions among men determined to observe truth in all their ways and words. I can understand a simple, ignorant rustic, who has never learned to read, doing all this at the command of a priest and under the eye of a squire. I can even understand persons doing this when the Reformation was in its dawn, and men had newly crept out of the darkness of Popery; but I cannot understand gracious, godly people, standing at the font to insult the all-gracious Father with vows and promises framed upon a fiction, and involving practical falsehood. How dare intelligent believers in Christ to utter words which they know in their conscience to be wickedly aside from truth? When I shall be able to understand the process by which gracious men so accommodate their consciences, even then I shall have a confirmed belief that the God of truth never did and never will confirm a spiritual blessing of the highest order in connection with the utterance of such false promises and untruthful vows. My brethren, does it not strike you that declarations so fictitious are not likely to be connected with a new birth wrought by the Spirit of truth?

I have not done with this point, I must take another case, and suppose the sponsors and others to be *ungodly*, and that is no hard supposition, for in many cases we know that godfathers and parents have no more thought of religion than that idolatrous hollowed stone around which they gather. When these sinners have taken their places, what are they about to say? Why, they are about to make the solemn vows I have already recounted in your hearing! Totally irreligious they are, but yet they promise for the baby what they never did, and never thought of doing for themselves—they promise on behalf of this child, "that he will renounce the devil and all his works, and constantly believe God's holy Word, and obediently keep his commandments." My brethren, do not think I speak severely here. Really I think there is something here to make mockery for devils. Let every honest man lament, that ever God's Church should tolerate such a thing as this, and that there should be found gracious people who will feel grieved because I, in all kindness of heart, rebuke the atrocity. Unregenerate sinners promising for a poor babe that he shall keep all God's holy commandments which they themselves wantonly break every day! How can anything but the longsuffering of God endure this? What! not speak against it? The very stones in the street might cry out against the infamy of wicked men and women promising that another should renounce the devil and all his works, while they themselves serve the devil and do his works with greediness! As a climax to all this, I am asked to believe that God accepts that wicked promise, and as the result of it, regenerates that child. You cannot believe in regeneration by this operation, whether saints or sinners are the performers. Take them to be godly, then they are wrong for doing what their conscience must condemn; view them as ungodly, and they are wrong for promising what they know they cannot perform; and in neither case can God accept such worship, much less infallibly append regeneration to such a baptism as this.

But you will say "Why do *you* cry out against it?" I cry out against it because I believe that baptism does not save the soul, and that *the preaching of it has a wrong and evil influence upon men*. We meet with persons who, when we tell them that they must be born again, assure us that they were born again when they were baptized. The number of these persons is increasing, fearfully increasing, until all grades of society are misled by this belief. How can any man stand up in his pulpit and say Ye must be born again to his congregation, when he has already assured them, by his own "unfeigned assent and consent" to it, that they are themselves, every one of them, born again in baptism. What is he to do with them? Why, my dear friends, the gospel then has no voice; they have rammed this ceremony down its throat and it cannot speak to rebuke sin. The man who has been baptized or sprinkled says, "I *am* saved, I *am* a member of Christ, a child of God, and an inheritor of the kingdom of heaven. Who are you, that you should rebuke *me*? Call *me* to repentance? Call *me* to a new life? What better life can I have? for I *am* a member of Christ—a part of Christ's body. What! rebuke *me*? I am a child of God. Cannot you see it in my face? No matter what my walk and conversation is, I am a child of God. Moreover, I am an inheritor of the kingdom of heaven. It is true, I drink and swear, and all that, but you know I am an inheritor of the kingdom of heaven, for when I die, though I live in constant sin, you will put me in the grave, and tell everybody that I died 'in sure and certain hope of the resurrection to eternal life.'"

Now, what can be the influence of such preaching as this upon our beloved England? Upon my dear and blessed country? What but the worst of ills? If I loved her not, but loved myself most, I might be silent here, but, loving England, I cannot and dare not; and having soon to render an account before my God, whose servant I hope I am, I must free myself from this evil as well as from every other, or else on my head may be the doom of souls.

Here let me bring in another point. It is a most fearful fact, that *in no age since the Reformation has Popery made such fearful strides in England as during the last few years*. I had comfortably believed that Popery was only feeding itself upon foreign subscriptions, upon a few titled perverts, and imported monks and nuns. I dreamed that its progress was not real. In fact, I have often smiled at the alarm of many of my brethren at the progress of Popery. But, my dear friends, we have been mistaken, grievously mistaken. If you will read a valuable paper in the magazine called "Christian Work," those of you who are not acquainted with it will be perfectly startled at its revelations. This great city is now covered with a network of monks, and priests, and sisters of mercy, and the conversions made are not by ones or twos, but by scores, till England is being regarded as the most hopeful spot for Romish missionary enterprise in the whole world; and at the present moment there is not a mission which is succeeding to anything like the extent which the English mission is. I covet not their money, I despise their sophistries, but I marvel at the way in which they gain their funds for the erection of their ecclesiastical buildings. It really is an alarming matter to see so many of our countrymen going off to that superstition which as a nation we once rejected, and which it was supposed we should never again receive. Popery is making advances such as you would never believe, though a spectator should tell it to you. Close to your very doors, perhaps even in your own houses, you may have evidence ere long of what a march Romanism is making. And to what is it to be ascribed? I say, with every ground of probability, that there is no marvel that Popery should increase when you have two things to make it grow: first of all, the falsehood of those who profess a faith which they do not believe, which is quite contrary to the honesty of the Romanist, who does through evil report and good report hold his faith; and then you have, secondly, this form of error known as baptismal regeneration, and commonly called Puseyism, which is not only Puseyism, but Church-of-Englandism, because it is in the Prayer Book, as plainly as words can express it—you have this baptismal regeneration preparing stepping-stones to make it easy for men to go to Rome. I have but to open my eyes a little to foresee Romanism rampant everywhere in the future, since its germs are spreading everywhere in the present. In one of our courts of legislature but last Tuesday, the Lord Chief Justice showed his superstition, by speaking of "the risk of the calamity of children dying unbaptized!" Among Dissenters you see a veneration for structures, a modified belief in the sacredness of places, which is idolatry; for to believe in the sacredness of anything but of God and of his own Word, is to idolize, whether it is to believe in the sacredness of the men, the priests, or in the sacredness of the bricks and mortar, or of the fine linen, or what not, which you may use in the worship of God. I see this coming up everywhere—a belief in ceremony, a resting in ceremony, a veneration for altars, fonts, and Churches—a veneration so profound that we must not venture upon a remark, or straightway of sinners we are chief. Here is the essence and soul of Popery, peeping up under the garb of a decent respect for sacred things. It is impossible but that the Church of Rome must spread, when we who are the watch-dogs of the fold are silent, and others are gently and smoothly turfing the road, and making it as soft and smooth as possible, that converts may travel down to the nethermost hell of Popery. We want John Knox back again. Do not talk to me of mild and gentle men, of soft manners and squeamish words, we want the fiery Knox, and even though his vehemence should "ding our pulpits into blads," it were well if he did but rouse our hearts to action. We want Luther to tell men the truth unmistakably, in homely phrase. The velvet has got into our ministers' mouths of late, but we must unrobe ourselves of soft raiment, and truth must be spoken, and nothing but truth; for of all lies which have dragged millions down to hell, I look upon this as being one of the most atrocious—that in a Protestant Church there should be found those who swear that baptism saves the soul. Call a man a Baptist, or a Presbyterian, or a Dissenter, or a Churchman, that is nothing to me—if he says that baptism saves the soul, out upon him, out upon him, he states what God never taught, what the Bible never laid down, and what ought never to be maintained by men who profess that the Bible, and the whole Bible, is the religion of Protestants.

I have spoken thus much, and there will be some who will say—spoken thus much bitterly. Very well, be it so. Physic is often bitter, but it shall work well, and the physician is not bitter because his medicine is so; or if he be accounted so, it will matter, so long as the patient is cured; at all events, it is no business of the patient whether the physician is bitter or not, his business is with his own soul's health. There is the truth, and I have told it to you; and if there should be one among you, or if there should be one among the readers of this sermon when it is printed, who is resting on baptism, or resting upon ceremonies of any sort, I do beseech you, shake off this venomous faith into the fire as Paul did the viper which fastened on his hand. I pray you do not rest on baptism.

"NO OUTWARD FORMS CAN MAKE YOU CLEAN, THE LEPROSY LIES DEEP WITHIN."

I do beseech you to remember that you must have a new heart and a right spirit, and baptism cannot give you these. You must turn from your sins and follow after Christ; you must have such a faith as shall make your life holy and your speech devout, or else you have not the faith of God's elect, and into God's kingdom you shall never come. I pray you never rest upon this wretched and rotten foundation, this deceitful invention of antichrist. O, may God save you from it, and bring you to seek the true rock of refuge for weary souls.

I come with much brevity, and I hope with much earnestness, in the second place, to say that FAITH IS THE INDISPENSABLE REQUISITE TO SALVATION. "He that *believeth* and is baptized shall be saved; he that *believeth* not shall be damned." Faith is the one indispensable requisite for salvation. This faith is the gift of God. It is the work of the Holy Spirit. Some men believe not on Jesus; they believe not because they are not of Christ's sheep, as he himself said unto them; but his sheep hear his voice: he knows them and they follow him: he gives to them eternal life, and they shall never perish, neither shall any pluck them out of his hand. What is this believing? Believing consists in two things; first there is *an accrediting of the testimony of God* concerning his Son. God tells you that his Son came into the world and was made flesh, that he lived upon earth for men's sake, that after having spent his life in holiness he was offered up a propitiation for sin, that upon the cross he there and then made expiation—so made expiation for the sins of the world that Whosoever believeth in him shall not perish, but have everlasting life. If you would be saved, you must accredit this testimony which God gives concerning his own Son. Having received this testimony, the next thing is to *confide in it*— indeed here lies, I think, the essence of saving faith, to rest yourself for eternal salvation upon the atonement and the righteousness of Jesus Christ, to have done once for all with all reliance upon feelings or upon doings, and to trust in Jesus Christ and in what he did for your salvation.

This is faith, receiving of the truth of Christ: first knowing it to be true, and then acting upon that belief. Such a faith as this—such real faith as this makes the man henceforth hate sin. How can he love the thing which made the Saviour bleed? It makes him live in holiness. How can he but seek to honour that God who has loved him so much as to give his Son to die for him. This faith is spiritual in its nature and effects; it operates upon the entire man; it changes his heart, enlightens his judgment, and subdues his will; it subjects him to God's supremacy, and makes him receive God's Word as a little child, willing to receive the truth upon the *ipse dixit* of the divine One; it sanctifies his intellect, and makes him willing to be taught God's Word; it cleanses within; it makes clean the inside of the cup and platter, and it beautifies without; it makes clean the exterior conduct and the inner motive, so that the man, if his faith be true and real, becomes henceforth another man to what he ever was before.

Now that such a faith as this should save the soul, is, I believe, reasonable; yea, more, it is certain, for *we have seen men saved by it* in this very house of prayer. We have seen the harlot lifted out of the Stygian ditch of her sin, and made an honest woman; we have seen the thief reclaimed; we have known the drunkard in hundreds of instances to be sobered; we have observed faith to work such a change, that all the neighbours who have seen it have gazed and admired, even though they hated it; we have seen faith deliver men in the hour of temptation, and help them to consecrate themselves and their substance to God; we have seen, and hope still to see yet more widely, deeds of heroic consecration to God and displays of witness-bearing against the common current of the times, which have proved to us that faith does affect the man, does save the soul. My hearers, if you would be saved, you must believe in the Lord Jesus Christ. Let me urge you with all my heart to look nowhere but to Christ crucified for your salvation. Oh! if you rest upon any ceremony, though it be not baptism—if you rest upon any other than Jesus Christ, you must perish, as surely as this Book is true. I pray you believe not every spirit, but though I, or an angel from heaven, preach any other doctrine than this, let him be accursed, for this, and this alone, is the soul-saving truth which shall regenerate the world—"He that believeth and is baptized shall be saved." Away from all the tag-rags, wax candles, and millinery of Puseyism! away from all the gorgeous pomp of Popery! away from the fonts of Church-of-Englandism! we bid you turn your eyes to that naked cross, where hangs as a bleeding man the Son of God.

"NONE BUT JESUS, NONE BUT JESUS
CAN DO HELPLESS SINNERS GOOD."

There is life in a look at the crucified; there is life at this moment for you. Whoever among you can believe in the great love of God towards man in Christ Jesus, you shall be saved. If you can believe that our great Father desireth us to come to him—that he panteth for us—that he calleth us every day with the loud voice of his Son's wounds; if you can believe now that in Christ there is pardon for transgressions past, and cleansing for years to come; if you can trust him to save you, you have already the marks of regeneration. The work of salvation is commenced in you, so far as the Spirit's work is concerned: it is finished in you so far as Christ's work is concerned. O, I would plead with you—lay hold on Jesus Christ. This is *the* foundation: build on it. This is *the* rock of refuge: fly to it. I pray you fly to it now. Life is short: time speeds with eagle's-wing. Swift as the dove pursued by the hawk, fly, fly poor sinner, to God's dear Son; now touch the hem of his garment; now look into that dear face, once marred with sorrows for you; look into those eyes, once shedding tears for you. Trust him, and if you find him false, then you must perish; but false you never will find him while this word standeth true, "He that believeth and is baptized shall be saved; but he that believeth not shall be damned." God give us this vital, essential faith, without which there is no salvation. Baptized, re-baptized, circumcised, confirmed, fed upon sacraments, and buried in consecrated ground—ye shall all perish except ye believe in him. The word is express and plain—he that believeth not may plead his baptism, may plead anything he likes, "But he that believeth not shall be damned;" for him there is nothing but the wrath of God, the flames of hell, eternal perdition. So Christ declares, and so must it be.

But now to close, there are some who say, "Ah! but baptism is in the text; where do you put that?" That shall be another point, and then we shall have done.

THE BAPTISM IN THE TEXT IS ONE EVIDENTLY CONNECTED WITH FAITH. "He that believeth and is baptized shall be saved." It strikes me, there is no supposition here, that anybody would be baptized who did not believe; or, if there be such a supposition, it is very clearly laid down that his baptism will be of no use to him, for he will be damned, baptized or not, unless he believes. The baptism of the text seems to me—my brethren, if you differ from me I am sorry for it, but I must hold my opinion and out with it—it seems to me that baptism is connected with, nay, directly follows belief. I would not insist too much upon the order of the words, but for other reasons, I think that baptism should follow believing. At any rate it effectually avoids the error we have been combating. A man who knows that he is saved by believing in Christ does not, when he is baptized, lift his baptism into a saving ordinance. In fact, he is the very best protester against that mistake, because he holds that he has no right to be baptized until he is saved. He bears a testimony against baptismal regeneration in his being baptized as professedly an already regenerate person. Brethren, the baptism here meant is a baptism connected with faith, and to this baptism I will admit there is very much ascribed in Scripture. Into that question I am not going; but I do find some very remarkable passages in which baptism is spoken of very strongly. I find this—"Arise, and be baptized, and wash away thy sins, calling on the name of the Lord." I find as much as this elsewhere; I know that believer's baptism itself does not wash away sin, yet it is so the outward sign and emblem of it to the believer, that the thing visible may be described as the thing signified. Just as our Saviour said—"This is my body," when it was not his body, but bread; yet, inasmuch as it represented his body, it was fair and right according to the usage of language to say, "Take, eat, this is my body." And so, inasmuch as baptism to the believer representeth the washing of sin—it may be called the washing of sin—not that it is so, but that it is to saved souls the outward symbol and representation of what is done by the power of the Holy Spirit, in the man who believes in Christ.

What connection has this baptism with faith? I think it has just this, *baptism is the avowal of faith;* the man was Christ's soldier, but now in baptism he puts on his regimentals. The man believed in Christ, but his faith remained between God and his own soul. In baptism he says to the baptizer, "I believe in Jesus Christ;" he says to the Church, "I unite with you as a believer in the common truths of Christianity;" he saith to the onlooker, "Whatever you may do, as for me, I will serve the Lord." It is the avowal of his faith.

Next, we think baptism is also to the believer a *testimony of his faith;* he does in baptism tell the world what he believes. "I am about," saith he, "to be buried in water. I believe that the Son of God was metaphorically baptized in suffering: I believe he was literally dead and buried." To rise again out of the water sets forth to all men that he believes in the resurrection of Christ. There is a showing forth in the Lord's Supper of Christ's death, and there is a showing forth in baptism of Christ's burial and resurrection. It is a type, a sign, a symbol, a mirror to the world: a looking-glass in which religion is as it were reflected. We say to the onlooker, when he asks what is the meaning of this ordinance, "We mean to set forth our faith that Christ was buried, and that he rose again from the dead, and we avow this death and resurrection to be the ground of our trust."

Again, baptism is also *Faith's taking her proper place*. It is, or should be one of her first acts of obedience. Reason looks at baptism, and says, "Perhaps there is nothing in it; it cannot do me any good." "True," says Faith, "and therefore will I observe it. If it did me some good my selfishness would make me do it, but inasmuch as to my sense there is no good in it, since I am bidden by my Lord thus to fulfil all righteousness, it is my first public declaration that a thing which looks to be unreasonable and seems to be unprofitable, being commanded by God, is law, is law to me. If my Master had told me to pick up six stones and lay them in a row I would do it, without demanding of him, 'What good will it do?' *Cui bono?* is no fit question for soldiers of Jesus. The very simplicity and apparent uselessness of the ordinance should make the believer say, 'Therefore I do it because it becomes the better test to me of my obedience to my Master.'" When you tell your servant to do something, and he cannot comprehend it, if he turns round and says, "Please, sir, what for?" you are quite clear that he hardly understands the relation between master and servant. So when God tells me to do a thing, if I say, "What for?" I cannot have taken the place which Faith ought to occupy, which is that of simple obedience to whatever the Lord hath said. Baptism is commanded, and Faith obeys because it is commanded, and thus takes her proper place.

Once more, *baptism is a refreshment to Faith*. While we are made up of body and soul as we are, we shall need some means by which the body shall sometimes be stirred up to co-work with the soul. In the Lord's Supper my faith is assisted by the outward and visible sign. In the bread and in the wine I see no superstitious mystery, I see nothing but bread and wine, but in that bread and wine I do see to my faith an assistant. Through the sign my faith sees the thing signified. So in baptism there is no mysterious efficacy in the baptistry or in the water. We attach no reverence to the one or to the other, but we do see in the water and in the baptism such an assistance as brings home to our faith most manifestly our being buried with Christ, and our rising again in newness of life with him. Explain baptism thus, dear friends, and there is no fear of Popery rising out of it. Explain it thus, and we cannot suppose any soul will be led to trust to it; but it takes its proper place among the ordinances of God's house. To lift it up in the other way, and say men are saved by it—ah! my friends, how much of mischief that one falsehood has done and may do, eternity alone will disclose. Would to God another George Fox would spring up in all his quaint simplicity and rude honesty to rebuke the idol-worship of this age; to rail at their holy bricks and mortar, holy lecterns, holy alters, holy surplices, right reverend fathers, and I know not what. These things are not holy. God is holy; his truth is holy; holiness belongs not to the carnal and the material, but to the spiritual. O that a trumpet-tongue would cry out against the superstition of the age. I cannot, as George Fox did, give up baptism and the Lord's Supper, but I would infinitely sooner do it, counting it the smaller mistake of the two than perpetrate and assist in perpetrating the uplifting of baptism and the Lord's Supper out of their proper place. O my beloved friends, the comrades of my struggles and witnessings, cling to the salvation of faith, and abhor the salvation of priests. If I am not mistaken, the day will come when we shall have to fight for a simple spiritual religion far more than we do now. We have been cultivating friendship with those who are either unscriptural in creed or else dishonest, who either believe baptismal regeneration, or profess that they do, and swear before God that they do when they do not. The time is come when there shall be no more truce or parley between God's servants and the time-servers. The time is come when those who follow God must follow God, and those who try to trim and dress themselves and find out a way which is pleasing to the flesh and gentle to carnal desires, must go their way. A great winnowing time is coming to God's saints, and we shall be clearer one of these days than we now are from union with those who are upholding Popery, under the pretence of teaching Protestantism. We shall be clear, I say, of those who teach salvation by baptism, instead of salvation by the blood of our blessed Master, Jesus Christ. O may the Lord gird up your loins. Believe me, it is no trifle. It may be that on this ground Armageddon shall be fought. Here shall come the great battle between Christ and his saints on the one hand, and the world, and forms, and ceremonies, on the other. If we are overcome here, there may be years of blood and persecution, and tossing to and fro between darkness and light; but if we are brave and bold, and flinch not here, but stand to God's truth, the future of England may be bright and glorious. O for a truly reformed Church in England, and a godly race to maintain it! The world's future depends on it under God, for in proportion as truth is marred at home, truth is maimed abroad. Out of any system which teaches salvation by baptism must spring infidelity, an infidelity which the false Church already seems willing to nourish and foster beneath her wing. God save this favoured land from the brood of her own established religion. Brethren, stand fast in the liberty wherewith Christ has made you free, and be not afraid of any sudden fear nor calamity when it cometh, for he who trusteth to the Lord, mercy shall compass him about, and he who is faithful to God and Christ shall hear it said at the last, "Well done, good and faithful servant, enter thou into the joy of the Lord."

May the Lord bless this word for Christ's sake.

3

Baptism Essential to Obedience

October 13, 1889
Metropolitan Tabernacle, Newington

"He who believes and is baptized shall be saved."

—Mark 16:16

IF OUR CONGREGATION WERE WHAT they ought to be, it would be a very simple matter to preach, for a sermon would then only need to be like the orders given by a commanding officer to his troops—short, sharp, plain, clear, distinct! Our hearers would not need illustrations and metaphors—they would simply ask to be told what they must do to be saved—and the more plainly they could be told, the better pleased would they be. I am going to try, this evening, to preach that kind of sermon, sinking the preacher into the teller of good news, plainly speaking of the way of salvation. If you want to be saved, listen to my message. If you do not care for salvation, yet, perhaps, while you hear it, you may be set a-longing, and God may bless you. My text is preceded and followed by other important words, "Go you into all the world and preach the Gospel to every creature. He who believes and is baptized shall be saved; but he that believes not shall be damned."

The Gospel, then, is for "every creature." Wherever there is a man, woman, or child—an intelligent creature—the Gospel is to be preached to such a person. You who are gathered tonight are clearly within that description and, therefore, the Gospel is to be preached to you. But if we are commanded to preach it, it is *implied* that you are commanded to *hear* it! To hear it without attention—to hear it without resolving to *obey* it—will be useless work. Hear it, therefore, as I desire to preach it, remembering that Christ stands here to hear me preach and to mark how you accept the message from Himself that I am to deliver.

This Gospel is sent to every creature because every creature needs it. Whether the creature knows it or not, he is lost—lost by nature and lost by practice, too—so much lost that he cannot save himself! He needs to be saved. Will you all believe that? If you have not believed in Christ, you are lost, and you cannot save yourself. Begin by believing that fact. But then rejoice that there is sent to you a Gospel which can save you, a Gospel which is adapted and meant for the salvation of just such a person as you are, for to you God says—"He who believes and is baptized shall be saved."

My fellow Christians, you who have believed in Christ, it is time for us to bestir ourselves, for we have not preached the Gospel to every creature, yet, by any stretch of the imagination! Some persons have never preached it to *anybody*—some, I mean, of the very persons who are commanded to preach it to every creature! A quaint preacher says that if some of God's people were paid ten dollars an hour for all that they have done for their Lord, they have not earned enough, yet, to buy a gingerbread cake, and I am afraid that statement is true. So very little have some persons done for the spread of the Gospel that the world is none the better for their being in it! Do I speak too severely? If I do, you can easily pass over what I say, but if not, if it is so that any here have never yet fairly and squarely spoken of the Gospel of Jesus Christ, begin at once!

When you get home, tonight, speak of the Gospel to your nearest relative, and go out, tomorrow, to your next door neighbor, or to the friend whom you can most easily reach, and tell them of the good news that your Lord has revealed to you, and so help to preach the Gospel to every creature! An army chaplain once said to the Duke of Wellington, "Do you think that it is of any use our taking the Gospel to the hill tribes in India? Will they ever receive it?" The duke replied, "What are your marching orders?" That was the only answer he gave! Stern disciplinarian as that great soldier was, he only needed marching orders and he obeyed—and he meant that every soldier of the Cross must obey the marching orders of Christ, his great Commander. Go you, therefore, as far as your position and capabilities allow you, and tell to every creature the word of the Gospel as it is recorded in my text, "He who believes and is baptized shall be saved."

I want to do my part, tonight, as far as my feeble voice will permit me. And I will speak a few words, first, *concerning belief.* Secondly, *concerning Baptism.* And, thirdly, *concerning being saved.* We shall get the whole text clearly in considering those three points.

I. First, CONCERNING BELIEVING. This is the main point. This is the hinge of salvation, for he that believes in Christ is not condemned—he that believes in Him has everlasting life. Now, concerning believing, let me, ask, first, *What is to be believed?* Well, you are to believe that you have broken the Law of God and that, consequently, you are under condemnation. But that God, in His infinite mercy, has sent His Son, Jesus

Christ, into the world that you might live through Him. His Divine Son—His only-begotten Son—was born of Mary, as a Man of the substance of His mother, feeling as we do and was, in all respects, most truly Man. Being here, He obeyed His Father's will and, when the time came, He gave Himself up as a Sacrifice for guilty men. He died, "the Just for the unjust, that He might bring us to God." Himself being without sin, He took upon Himself the sin of His people— "Who His own self bore our sins in His own body on the tree." Being found with human sin imputed to Him, He suffered in the place of those whose sins He bore. On the Cross His blood was shed—for without the shedding of blood there is no remission of sin—and by that shedding of blood He blotted out the iniquity of all those who put their trust in Him. This is what you have to believe, that—

"HE BORE, THAT YOU MIGHT NEVER BEAR, HIS FATHER'S RIGHTEOUS IRE."

He was laid in the grave and on the third day He came forth from the tomb, rising, again, for the justification of His people as He was crucified for their offenses. After a while He went up into the highest Heaven and He is now enthroned there, King of Kings, and Lord of Lords. He sits at the right hand of God, even the Father, and there He pleads and makes intercession for sinners. Believe this—"Through this Man is preached unto you the forgiveness of sins." He is exalted on high, a Prince and a Savior, to give repentance and remission of sins. That is what is to be believed. I might go into a great many details, but I shall not do so tonight. The essence of what is to be believed is that Jesus Christ is given of God unto us, that by His death He might put away sin and we might be reconciled to God—and that *whoever* believes in Him shall not perish, but have everlasting life!

That I may answer this question better, let me correct it, or turn it into another, and then answer that. The question is not so much what is to be believed, as *Who is to be believed?* For, in very deed, the believing of a certain thing to be true, though that may be helpful, is not the whole of the matter. I, believing a thing to be true, trust myself to that truth—there is *faith*, the act of *trust*. But if we would be saved, we must trust a Person! We must trust the Lord Jesus Christ. You are not so much saved by believing a doctrine as by *trusting* a Person—you must believe the dogma, or you will not trust the Person, but, believing the doctrine, you then come, and put your trust in the Person about whom that doctrine is taught. If you would be saved, trust yourself with Jesus Christ! He, who died, lives, and, "He is able to save unto the uttermost them that come unto God by Him." Saving faith is trusting in the Lord Jesus Christ—trusting Him truly, wholly, solely, constantly—trusting Him now! Behold Him, then, the Son of God, enthroned in Glory! Lay your soul and all its sins at His dear feet and trust in Him to save you—and He will do it!

Many will ask a third question—*Why is He to be trusted?* I should like to answer that by another—Why is He *not* to be trusted? When one said to me, the other day, "I cannot trust Christ," I enquired, "Can you trust *me?*" And when the quick reply was, as it ought to be from a hearer to a minister, "Yes, Sir, I do trust you," I said, "Well, then, you certainly can trust the Lord Jesus Christ, for He is infinitely more worthy of being trusted than ever I can be." Cannot trust Christ? That is a wonderful piece of Satanic delusion! I can say, tonight, that I can not only trust my soul to Christ, but that if I had as many souls as there are grains of sand on the seashore, I could implicitly trust them all to Him! Why should I not? He is "God over all, blessed forever," and He is Man, tender and gentle—therefore He ought to be trusted. O my Hearer, can you look the Crucified Christ in the face and say that you cannot trust Him? Can you see the bloody sweat in the garden? Can you gaze upon the nailed hands and feet and pierced side of this suffering Man, who is, at the same time, very God of very God, and can you then say that it is hard to trust Him? Oh, no! He is so true, so noble, so generous, so faithful that I beseech you to trust Him, and to trust Him now!

That raises another question—*When is Christ to be trusted?* And the answer is, NOW! He was never more worthy to be trusted than He is tonight and you never more needed a Savior than you do tonight. You are, perhaps, talking about trusting Christ at some future time. You tell me that you do not trust So-and-So, but that you hope to trust him one of these days. I will not give a penny for such a hope as that! No, Friend, if at any future time you should deem Christ worthy of your confidence, He is worthy of your trust, tonight, for He is the same yesterday, today and forever. Just as you are, in that pew, or sitting in the aisle, Christ deserves your confidence—and I pray you to give it to Him. Cast your guilty soul on Him this very moment! Live not another second in unbelief, for that unbelief is a slander on my Lord, a grievous injury to His dear, faithful love. Now, while the word is leaving my lips—as it reaches your ears—say and mean it, "I do believe. I will trust Jesus. I yield myself to Christ and take Him to be my Savior."

"If I do that," says one, "*When will the blessing come?*" The text says, "He who believes and is baptized shall be saved," and the blessing will come at once! Swift as the lightning flash is the act which saves the soul! One moment a man may be black with accumulated sin—the next moment he may be white as the driven snow. It takes no time for God to blot out iniquity. We pass in an instant from death to life, from darkness into marvelous light! I am praying that while I speak to you in feebleness, God may work with His almighty power—with that right hand that tore the Red Sea in two—that the ransomed of the Lord might cross over dry-shod! May He come and save the people made ready by His Grace for this night of His glorious power, leading them immediately to believe and giving them, at once, as the result of their faith, reconciliation to God and justification by Christ Jesus!

Here let me correct a mistake into which some people fall. They say, "Do you exhort us to believe?" I do, indeed, with all my heart. "But, Sir, faith is the work of the Spirit of God." Yes, did I ever say that it was not? I insist upon it continually that, wherever there is any faith, it is worked in us by the Spirit of God. But listen. Did I ever tell you the Spirit of God believed *for* us, or did you ever read anything in Scripture approximating to that statement? No, the Spirit of God *leads* us to believe, but we distinctly believe—and it is our faith that saves us—it is not that the Holy Spirit believes instead of us and we lie still, like a man under the surgeon's knife. Oh, dear, no! Every faculty is awakened and awakened by the Spirit of God! We see that Christ can save and we believe it. We believe that He will save and we trust Him to save us. It is our own act and deed—it cannot be anybody else's act and deed. You cannot believe for another! There can be nothing like sponsorship, here, and the Holy Spirit, Himself, cannot believe for you! It is not written, "Let the Holy Spirit believe for you." That would be absurd! But it *is* written, "Believe you." "Believe on the Lord Jesus Christ, and you shall be saved." With your own proper mind and heart you must believe in Jesus Christ if you would be saved.

I do not know that I need say more concerning believing. I have often tried to explain it, but I am afraid that I have not always made it as plain as I have intended. Only let me warn you *not* to say, "I understand the plan of salvation very well. Dear Sir, I am sure I do! I do not need it explained to me, I understand it perfectly." My dear Friend, it is one thing to understand the *plan* of salvation and quite another thing to *believe in Jesus Christ to the salvation of your soul.* It is a pitiless night, the rain is pouring down and here is a man, sitting out in the street, exposed to the ill weather, and he has got a plan of a house down there on the wet pavement. And He says, "I am all right! I understand the plan of a house quite well." You see, he is looking at the *plan*—he has a view of the front of the house—he knows where the windows and doors should be. And he has a ground plan, too! He can see where the kitchen is and the passage to the kitchen. And he knows the arrangement of all the rooms. But, my dear Fellow, you are getting wet through and through from the raging storm—why do you not go into the house for shelter? "Do not talk to me," he says, "I understand the plan of a house very well." The man is a fool if he talks like that! Everybody concludes that he is out of his mind and what is he who is satisfied with understanding the plan of salvation, but who does not come to Christ and put his trust in Him? Come to Him now, I beseech you! You who do not know so much about the plan of salvation, come to Jesus—come and trust Him—trust Him now!

II. Now, in the second place, a little CONCERNING BAPTISM—"He who believes and is baptized shall be saved."

Please observe that I did not make the text. Perhaps if I had made it, I should have left out that piece about Baptism—but I have had no hand in making the Bible—I am obliged to take God's Word as I find it. And here I read these words of our Lord Jesus Christ, "He who believes and is baptized shall be saved." "Do not dwell on the Baptism," says one—"leave that out." That is what *you* say, my dear Sir. I cannot see your face, but I do not believe that you are my master. My Master is the Lord who taught holy men to write this Book and I can only go by the Book! The Book has the Baptism in it, so I must stick to the Truth of God as it is in the Book—"He who believes and is baptized shall be saved."

First, let me remind you that our Savior's words teach us that *Baptism follows faith*—"He who believes and is baptized." Never neglect the order of things in the Bible! If God puts them one, two, three—do not you put them three, two, one. You never had a servant, I hope, who twisted your orders out of order. Did you ever say to her, "Mary, now go and sweep the parlor, and afterwards take the duster and dust the table, and the shelves and the books"? Did she come to you, some time later, and say, "Madam, I have done as you commanded me. I dusted the table, the shelves and the books, and then I swept the room"? Every good housewife here knows what would happen from turning the orders upside down in that fashion!

Now, a great many in the Christian Church at the present day have put it thus—"He that is baptized and believes." I am not one of those

45

maidservants. I dare not turn my Master's orders upside down! You have no right to baptize people till they have believed in Christ as their Savior. Remember how Philip put it to the Ethiopian eunuch when that worthy man said, "See, here is water; what does hinder me to be baptized?" Philip answered, "If you believe with all your heart, you may." And if you do not believe with all your heart, you ought not to be baptized—you have no right to this ordinance of Christ unless you are a Christian! "He who believes and is baptized"—that is the Scriptural order. Read the New Testament impartially and you will always find that those who were baptized were Believers. They believed in the Lord Jesus Christ and *then* they were baptized into the name of the Father, and of the Son, and of the Holy Spirit.

Next, I would have you notice that this matter of *Baptism is often linked with faith.* Over and over again it is put so in the New Testament! There are passages which I will not quote tonight, in which Baptism has a peculiar prominence given to it in connection with the work of salvation. It might have been put, "He who believes and comes to the Communion Table shall be saved," but it is not so written. Some churches have exalted what they call, "The Holy Eucharist," into a very elevated position, indeed—far beyond what Scripture has ever accorded to it—yet the Lord's Supper has never had given to it in the Word of God the position of being put side by side with faith as Baptism is in this and other passages. I am not going to dwell upon that point, tonight. I merely tell you what is the teaching of the New Testament. You shall give your own account of it if you please, but our appeal is, "to the Law and to the Testimony!"

This much, also, I must say, that *it is not possible that there can be anything saving in the Baptism, itself.* The act of applying water in anyway whatever cannot wash away a single sin! That would be going back to the old Covenant of Works, the old ceremonies of the Mosaic Law. All the washings under the law—and they were very many—never washed one sin away! Nor can any washing in water take away the sin of any man. Even the tears of Christ are never spoken of as putting away sin—it is His precious *blood*, alone, that cleanses away the sin of men. In my text, while it says, "He who believes and is baptized shall be saved," yet, when the condemnation is announced, it is simply, "He who *believes not* shall be damned," and the matter of Baptism is not mentioned, for there are many who believe, but who are not baptized, and who cannot be—as the dying thief, for instance—yet are they assuredly saved. Nevertheless, here stands my text and I cannot alter it, "He who believes and is baptized shall be saved."

Why do you suppose that Baptism is put into this prominent position? I think that it is for this reason—*Baptism is the outward expression of the inward faith.* He who believes in Christ with his heart confesses his faith before God and before the Church of God by being baptized. Now, the faith that speaks thus is not a dumb faith. It is not a cowardly faith. It is not a sneaking faith. Paul puts the matter thus, "If you shall confess with your mouth the Lord Jesus, and shall believe in your heart that God has raised Him from the dead, you shall be saved. For with the heart man believes unto righteousness and with the mouth confession is made unto salvation."

But why is confession so necessary to prove true faith? I answer that it is necessary to the very existence of the Church of God, for, if I may be a Believer and never confess my faith, you may be a Believer and never confess your faith—and all round we should thus have a company of men believing, but none of them confessing! And where would be the outward ordinances of the Church of Christ at all? Where would be any minister? Where would be the setting up and growing of the Kingdom of Christ? For a hundred reasons, it is absolutely necessary for Christ's Kingdom that the Believer should openly confess his faith. Do you not see that? And therefore, Baptism being *God's way of our openly confessing our faith,* He requires it to be added to faith that the faith may be a *confessing* faith, not a cowardly faith—that the faith may be an open faith, not a private faith—that so the faith may be a working faith, influencing our life and the life of others, and not a mere secret attempt for self-salvation by a silent faith which dares not acknowledge Christ. Remember those words of the Lord Jesus, "Whoever, therefore, shall confess Me before men, Him will I confess, also, before My Father which is in Heaven. But whoever shall deny Me," (and in that place it means, "He who does not confess Me"), "before men, him will I also deny before My Father which is in Heaven." There is, therefore, no regenerating efficacy about water, or about immersion, or about Baptism in any shape or form—but it is necessary as the outward visible expression of the inward spiritual faith by which the soul is saved!

And, dear Friends, once more, *Baptism is often the test of obedience.* He who believes in Christ takes Him to be his Master as well as his Savior. And Christ, therefore, says to him, "Go and do so-and-so." If the man refuses to do it, he thereby proves that he does not intend to be the disciple of the Master. "Oh!" says one, "you know that Baptism is a nonessential." Have I not begged you to cease such idle and wicked talk as that? Have you a servant? Do you go to business early in the morning? Do you like a cup of tea at six o'clock, before you start for the city? The maid does not bring it

47

to you and you ask, "Why have I not had my tea brought to me?" "Oh," she answers, "it is non-essential. You can do your business very well without that cup of tea." Let such a reply as that be repeated, or let it be given only once, and I will tell you what will be non-essential! It will be non-essential for you to keep that girl any longer in your house! You will want another servant, for you will say, "Clearly she is no servant of mine! She sets herself up as the mistress of the house, for she begins to judge my commands and to say that this one is essential, and that one is not essential."

What do you mean by, "non-essential"? "I mean that I can be saved without being baptized." Will you dare to say that wicked sentence over again? "I mean that I can be saved without being baptized." You evil creature! So you will do nothing that Christ commands if you can be saved without doing it? You are hardly worth saving at all! A man who always needs to be paid for what he does—whose one idea of religion is that he will do what is essential to his own salvation—only cares to save his own skin and insinuates Christ may go where He likes! Clearly, you are no servant of His! You need to be saved from such a disreputable, miserable state of mind—and may the Lord save you!

Oftentimes, I believe that this little matter of Believers' Baptism is the test of the sincerity of our profession of love to Him. It would have been all the same, it may be, if the Lord Jesus Christ had said, "Pick up six stones off the ground and carry them in your pocket and you shall be saved." Somebody would have said, "That stone-picking is a non-essential." It becomes essential as soon as Christ commands it! It is in this way that Baptism, if not essential to your salvation, is essential to your *obedience* to Christ. If you have become His disciple, you are bound to obey all your Master's commands—"Whatever He says unto you, do it."

III. Now, lastly, CONCERNING BEING SAVED—"He who believes and is baptized shall be saved."

What is this being saved? Well, it means, of course, what everyone wants it to mean, *salvation from the punishment of sin.* "He who believes and is baptized shall be saved." His transgressions shall be forgiven him, his iniquity shall be blotted out, he shall not be brought into condemnation—and in the Last Great Day he shall be justified in Christ. No, he is justified *now*, as the Apostle says, "Therefore, being justified by faith, we have peace with God through our Lord Jesus Christ." That is certainly a part of this being saved.

It means, next, that he that believes and is baptized shall have *salvation from the dominion of his old nature*. When you believe in Christ, there shall suddenly spring up in you a new life, a new principle—a well shall be dug within your being and a fountain of Living Water shall begin to bubble up within you unto life everlasting! A miracle shall be worked upon you—there shall come into your heart the Holy Spirit who shall dwell there to re-create you, to set up within your soul a new throne whereon shall reign a new King! The old dominion of sin shall be broken as with a rod of iron and there shall be a new order of things within your heart—righteousness shall begin to reign there by Jesus Christ.

"He who believes and is baptized shall be saved." That is, he shall have *salvation from his old sins*. He shall no longer be the slave of drunkenness. He shall get the love of swearing by the throat. He shall have his lying, his anger, his passion under his feet. "He who believes and is baptized" shall see all his old adversaries put to the rout and what he could not do, through the weakness of his flesh, shall be done for him by the power of the Spirit of God! And by Divine Grace he shall master his sins. He shall begin to live unto God, under new impulses, strengthened with a new power and so he shall be delivered from his old sins.

Listen again, for this is wonderful. "He who believes and is baptized shall be saved"—he shall have *salvation from going back to his old sins*. If it were not for the Final Perseverance of the Saints, I should think my Gospel a poor Gospel to preach, but he who truly believes in Christ shall have such a change worked in him that the blessed work shall never be undone! My Lord shall light such a candle in your heart that the devil, himself, shall never be able to blow it out! Christ shall come to you with such power and authority and set up His eternal Throne in your soul with such Divine majesty and might that you shall be His in time and throughout eternity. We preach about no temporary salvation, no work of Grace that, by-and-by, will grow feeble and lose its power! We tell of a work of Grace that shall enable you who believe to go on from strength to strength, from glory to glory, till every sin in you shall be driven out and you shall be made perfectly like your Lord! Then shall you behold His face in righteousness and be with Him forever and ever.

Once more, "He who believes and is baptized shall be saved"—he shall have *salvation from the age in which he lives*. "But," says one, "I do not want to be saved from *that*." You don't? "No." But if you go with the age and go with the world, you will go down the Niagara which this age is just now shooting—down to the destruction to which this world is doomed!

Cherish not the friendship of the world that slew your Lord, for the world and the works that are in it shall be burned up. You remember how Peter said, on the day of Pentecost, "Save yourselves from this untoward generation"? That is what I want you to do tonight! "With many other words did he testify and exhort, saying, "Save yourselves from this untoward generation." A man who wishes to be a man and who desires to be a *saved* man, has to take up arms against this evil age! He who would prove himself to be alive unto God must swim against the current of the times! Dead fish go down stream—can't you see them? I see the white bellies of the dead fish floating down by myriads! But the living fish goes up the stream, against the current, and finds his way to purer waters! Beloved, he who believes in Jesus Christ with all his heart shall be made to play the man where men are now so few—and to stand fast for God and His Truth where others yield to the Satanic power—and to be holy where ungodliness, like a mighty torrent, now sweeps down our streets! "He who believes and is baptized" into the adorable name of Jesus, swears, as a Red Cross Knight, to follow Christ, and Christ, alone—believing in Him though every man is a liar—and resolving for Him to live, for Him to die and in Him to find hope here and eternal happiness hereafter! He is the man who shall be saved from this present evil age to the Glory of God the Father.

All this great work is worked by faith in Christ—that is the one way of salvation! "He who believes on the Son has everlasting life." Believe in Him, as men sometimes say, "up to the hilt." Believe in His Manhood sympathizing with you. Believe in His Godhead able to help you. Believe in His blood cleansing you. Believe in His eternal life bringing everlasting life to you. God bless you, everyone, for His dear Son's sake! Amen.

Exposition of John 3:1–18

If you were called in to see a person who was dying and wished to read a chapter from the Word of God, but you were afraid that the sick one did not know the way of salvation, you could not select a better portion than the one we are about to read. I have chosen it in the hope that some may now learn from it what they must do to be saved.

Verses 1, 2. *There was a man of the Pharisees named Nicodemus, a ruler of the Jews: the same came to Jesus by night.* Perhaps he was very busy during the day. It is better to come to Jesus at night than not to come to Him at all. All hours are convenient to Christ—you may come to Him when you are at home tonight. When everybody else is asleep, Jesus is still awake. In all probability, however, Nicodemus did not wish to commit himself by coming to Christ by day. He had not yet tried and tested Him, so he would not be thought to be Christ's follower till he had, first, had a quiet private talk with Him. As a ruler of the Jews, he was wise in acting thus discreetly.

2. *And said unto Him, Rabbi, we know that You are a teacher come from God: for no man can do these miracles that You do, except God is with him.* He admitted the truth as far as he could see it. The miracles of Christ proved Him to be a Divinely-commissioned teacher. Always be willing to go as far as you can go in the pursuit of the Truth of God. If you cannot see everything at once, see all that you can see. Be not of a caviling spirit—be frank and teachable as this man was.

3. *Jesus answered and said unto him, Verily, verily, I say unto you, Except a man is born again, he cannot see the Kingdom of God.* It is such a mystery, a thing of such a marvelous character, that his old nature cannot see it. He must have new eyes. He must be a new man. He must be born again before he can "see the Kingdom of God." Have you caught this idea, my dear Hearer? Do you understand that you cannot polish yourself up to a certain point and then see the Kingdom of God? You *must* be born again! There must be a radical change in you, a new birth, a birth from above, if you are even to *see* the Kingdom of God.

4, 5. *Nicodemus said unto Him, How can a man be born, when he is old? Can he enter the second time into his mother's womb and be born? Jesus answered, Verily, verily, I say unto you, Except a man is born of water and of the Spirit, he cannot enter into the kingdom of God.* At first Jesus said that a man could not *see* the kingdom of God except he was born again. Now He tells Nicodemus that a man cannot *enter* the Kingdom except he is born of water and of the Spirit. There must be a cleansing—he must be "born of water." There must be a spiritual life—he must be "born of the Spirit," or he cannot enter into the Kingdom of God.

6. *That which is born of the flesh is flesh.* Nothing more. However godly your father, however gracious your mother, all that is "born of the flesh is flesh."

6. *And that which is born of the spirit is spirit.* There must be, then, a Spirit-birth, or else you have no spirit—you belong not to the spiritual realm—and you cannot see and you cannot enter the *spiritual* Kingdom.

7, 8. *Marvel not that I said unto you, You must be born again. The wind blows where it wishes, and you hear the sound thereof.* The sounding of the wind blowing through the trees—

8. *But cannot tell from where it comes, and where it goes.* Where it begins, where it goes, or where it comes to an end, you cannot tell.

8. *So is everyone that is born of the Spirit.* You do not know where the spirit-life begins and you cannot tell to what it will lead. There are heights to which the spirit-life can carry you, of which you have never dreamed—this is a mystery beyond your understanding.

9. *Nicodemus answered and said unto Him, How can these things be?* He did not deny that they might be, but he asked how they could be. Ah, many a man has asked the same question! "How may I be made anew? How may I become a new creature?" Only He that makes all things can make all things new! The new birth is as great a wonder as creation, itself, and there is as much—and a great deal more—to be worked upon you to make you a Christian as has been worked upon you to make you a man.

10. *Jesus answered and said unto him, Are you a master of Israel, and know not these things?* These truths lie on the very doorstep of our holy religion! There are deeper and higher mysteries than these.

11, 12. *Verily, verily, I say unto you, We speak what We know, and testify what We have seen; and you receive not Our witness. If I have told you earthly things.* Commonplace things, the lower things of faith. "If I have told you these"—

12. *And you believe not, how shall you believe if I tell you of heavenly things?* There are mysteries in our holy religion which we would not tell to everybody. It would be casting pearls before swine to mention them to unregenerate men. Christ tells Nicodemus that the primary Truths of God must be believed before the more advanced doctrines can be revealed.

13. *And no man has ascended up to Heaven but He that came down from Heaven, even the Son of Man which is in Heaven.* It is Christ who knows everything! He understands all mysteries! He can teach all Truth, for He has been in Heaven. He came down to earth and He has gone back again to Heaven. Now, perhaps, some of you will be saying, "How are we to be saved? If there is no salvation without the new birth, how can we obtain the new birth?" Listen. The same chapter which tells you of the mystery of regeneration, tells you of the simple way of salvation by faith in Christ!

14, 15. *And as Moses lifted up the serpent in the wilderness, even so must the Son of Man be lifted up: that whoever believes in Him should not perish, but have eternal life.* "Whoever." If you believe in Christ, you are born again! If you trust Him, you have the new life! This simple way of salvation is not contradictory to the way of salvation by the new birth—it is the *same thing* stated in a form that we can comprehend!

16. *For God so loved the world, that He gave His only begotten Son, that whoever believes in Him should not perish, but have everlasting life.* This text has saved thousands of souls! The constellation in the heavens called the Great Bear, has in it the two pointers which direct the eyes of the observer to the pole star—and this verse points to Christ so clearly, so distinctly, that many have found Him by it and have lived! Let me read it again: "For God so loved the world, that He gave His only begotten Son, that whoever believes in Him should not perish, but have everlasting life."

17, 18. *For God sent not His Son into the world to condemn the world; but that the world, through Him, might be saved. He who believes on Him is not condemned: but He that believes not is condemned already.* Not, "shall be condemned at the last," though that, also, is true, but "He that believes not is condemned already"—

18. *Because he has not believed in the name of the only begotten Son of God.*

May the Lord bless to us the reading of this very simple Gospel chapter, for our Lord Jesus Christ's sake! Amen.

19205464R00032

Printed in Poland
by Amazon Fulfillment
Poland Sp. z o.o., Wrocław